The Hidden Heart Series
"Family"

Copyright © 2014 by Cindy Dahl
All rights reserved
www.cindydahl2007.wordpress.com

Art by Shaun Crum

ISBN-13: 978-1-941030-11-0

FAMILY

By Cindy Dahl

Illustrated By Shaun Crum

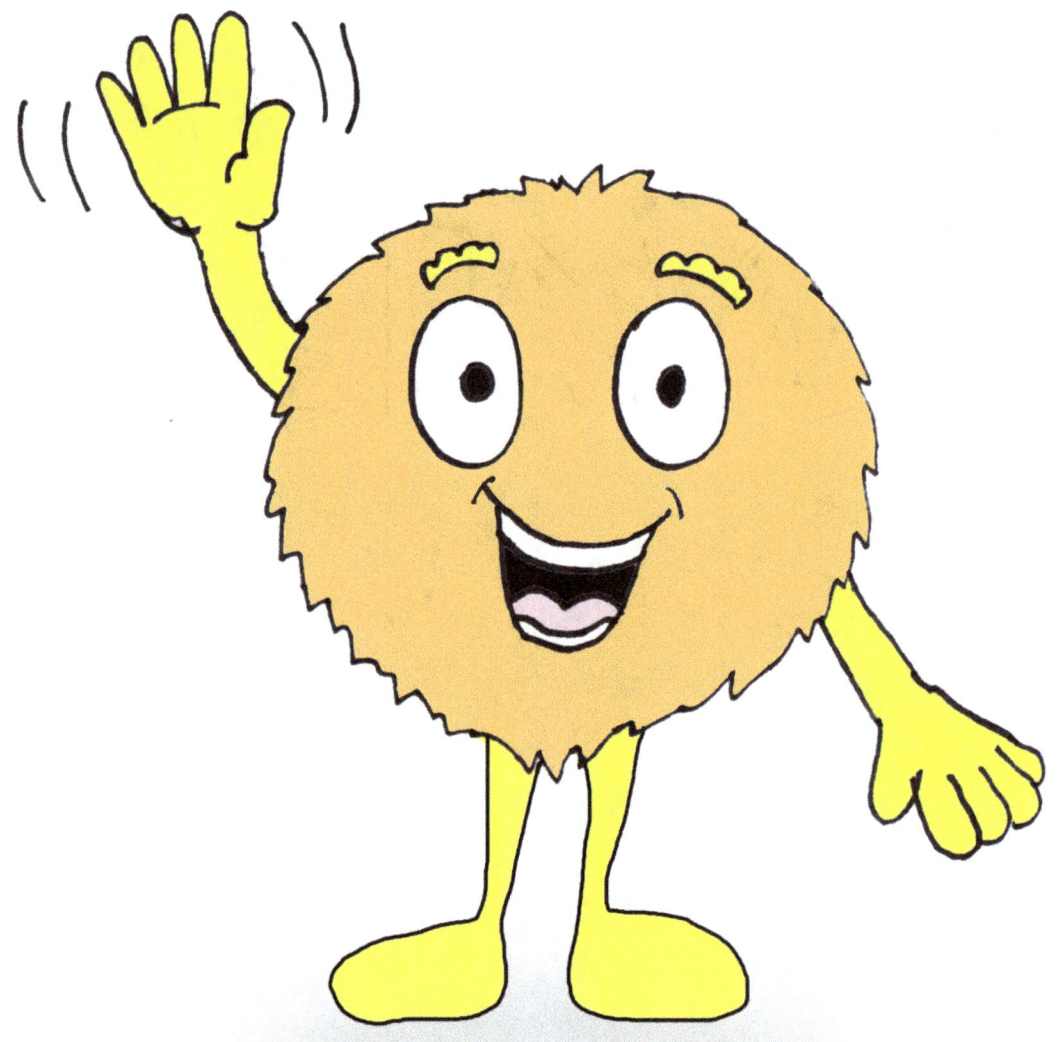

Hi, I am a GLíCK. You say it like /glēk/.
It stands for Giving, Loving, Inspiring, Caring and Kind. My books will show you how to be a GLíCK just like me!
I have hidden a heart in one of the pages; see if you can find the love in this book.

Hint: The hidden heart is on a tree behind a picnic table.

Family is so different
For every kid I know.
The important thing about family
Is the love they show.

Families help teach us
Who we want to be.
They teach us right from wrong
And take care of us lovingly.

You may have a Mom and Dad
Or maybe one or the other.
It really doesn't matter
When you love one another.

If you have two Moms
I would say you're blessed.
Two Dads would be the same,
As they hold you to their chest.

Lots of kids have Siblings;
Sisters or Brothers.
Some kids don't have ANY
But may have lots of others.

Being an only child
Doesn't mean you're alone.
You have friends and family
And toys all your own.

Just remember with a sibling
They will be family forever.
Friends may come and go
But a Brother or Sister - never.

What if your Mom or Dad
Married someone with a child?
That would be your step sibling,
Which is fun and kind of wild.

Having a step sibling
Might be hard at first.
But once you open your heart
You'll find it might just burst.

Some may think it's tough
To have a step Mom or Dad,
But with a special person
It can be the best you've ever had.

A Grandma and a Grandpa
Can be a lot of fun.
They're your Parent's Parents.
Sometimes there's only one.

You can call them different names.
Some are hard to top,
Like G-Ma or Nana
Or Papa or Granpop.

No matter what you call them
They will love you all the same.
They are special to your family
And may have your last name.

Maybe you have an Aunt;
Your Mom or Dad's Sister.
You may find she's cool
When you go out with her.

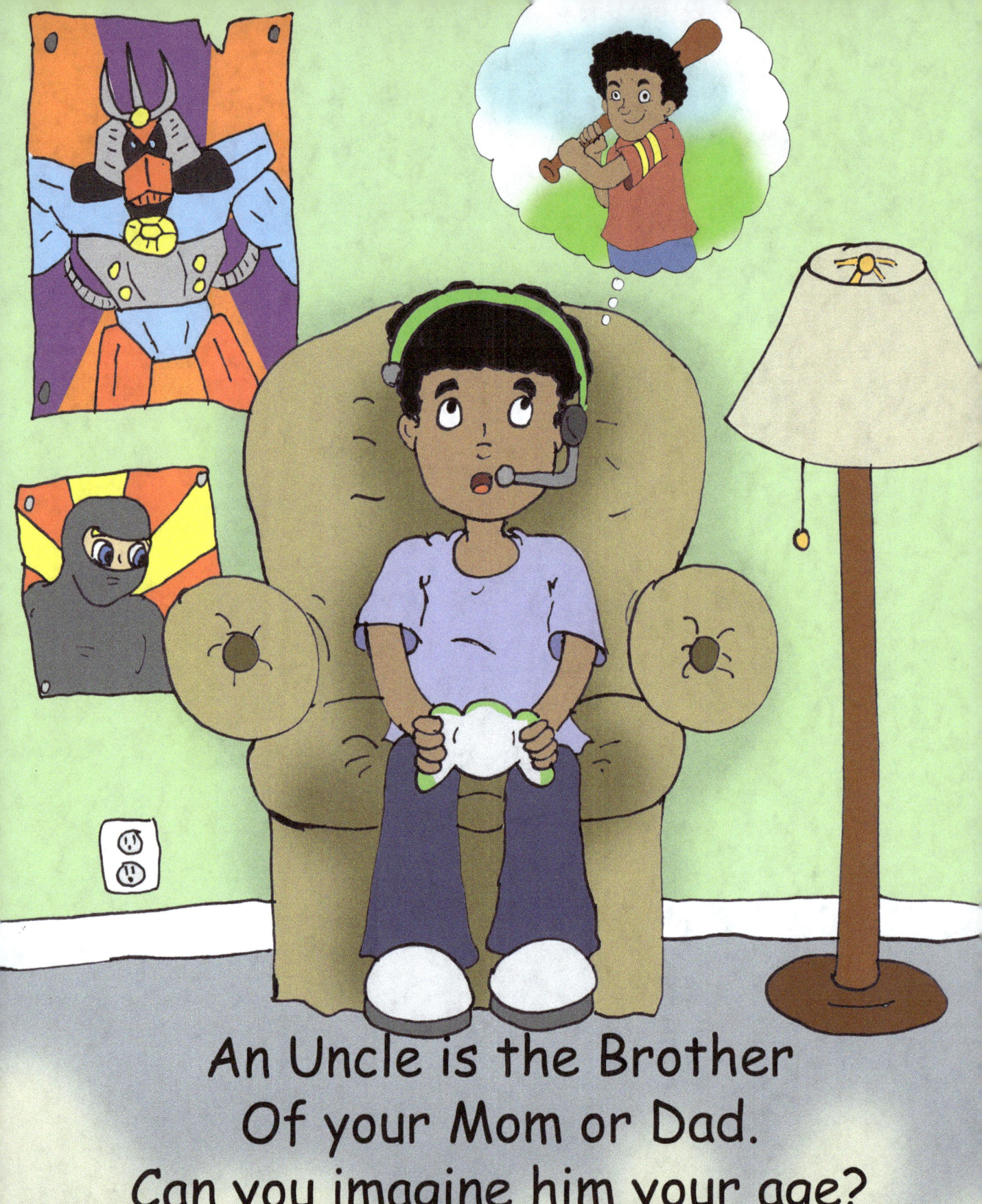

An Uncle is the Brother
Of your Mom or Dad.
Can you imagine him your age?
How he played or what he had?

It can get confusing
With so many in your family.
Remembering their names
Can be a struggle, sadly.

But where it can get crazy
Is when it comes to Cousins.
Some may have a few
While others may have dozens.

If your brother or sister
Ever had a baby,
You'd have a niece or nephew;
They'd look like you, maybe.

Animals are family
Like a special dog or cat.
They give you all their love
No matter where you're at.

So think of all your family,
Including closest friends.
The people you hold dearest
With the love that never ends.

Some families are really big
And others really small.
But as long as there is love
There is family for us all!

"When everything goes to heck,
the people who stand by you,
without flinching -- they are your family."
— Jim Butcher

Cindy Dahl is the author of several feel good children's books including the entire "hidden heart series" where kids get to find the hidden heart in each book. "It's like finding the love in the pages of a book." Cindy's main goal with writing her books is to inspire and bring a positive message for kids at a very young age. "It is never too young to learn to be kind to one another, to feel good about yourself, and to share with others."

Cindy grew up on a farm in Northern California and currently resides in Colorado. Cindy has three grown children. She read to them often when they were young and loved watching their faces when they felt the story come alive. In her spare time, Cindy enjoys being in the great Colorado outdoors.

www.ingramcontent.com/pod-product-compliance
Lightning Source LLC
Chambersburg PA
CBHW081732290426
43661CB00125B/869